STRANGE MEADOWLARK

STRANGE MEADOWLARK

Poems

MICHAEL SIMMS

Ragged Sky Press
Princeton, New Jersey

Published by Ragged Sky Press
270 Griggs Drive, Princeton, NJ 08540
www.raggedsky.com
Library of Congress Control Number: 2023935799
ISBN: 978-1-933974-53-8
Cover and book design: Pamela L. Schnitter
Cover photo: Eva-Maria Simms, Graffiti, artist unknown,
    Washington, DC, 2017
Printed in the United States of America
First Edition

Books by Michael Simms

Poetry
 Nightjar
 American Ash
 Migration

Novels
 The Green Mage
 Bicycles of the Gods: A Divine Comedy

Chapbooks of Poetry
 Black Stone
 The Happiness of Animals
 The Fire-eater
 Notes on Continuing Light

Textbooks with Jack Myers
 Dictionary of Poetic Terms
 Longman Dictionary and Handbook of Poetry

Contents

I

The Artist's Garden at Giverny   3
Zed   6
Against Prayer   7
Scarecrow   8
Imperfect   9
Leaving Walden   10
Odysseus in Hell   11
ω!   14
Ushant (Conrad Aiken at His Desk)   16
Strange Meadowlark   17
A Cowboy in the Chapel of Bones   20

II

Moon Pie and a Fanta   25
Prayer to St. Anthony   26
Thinking of the Rapture at Castriota Metals and Recycling   28
White Rock Lake   29
You Visit More Often Now That You're Dead   31
The Cold   33
The Cove   34
Wave   35
Trust   37
Breath   39

III

America   43
Night School   44
How My Brother Tried to Save Us   47
No   49
Hall of Blood   50
The Machinery   51
The Sentence   52
Brotherly Love   53

I V

Faye Donnelly Explains Why the Dead Are in Our Lives   59

V

Waterfall   69
Universal Beauty   71
Sidewalk Drain with Moss and String   72
The Simple Heart   73
Joy   74
Jubilate   75
Pupa (a meditation on becoming)   77
Coda: The Crows   82

Notes   83
Acknowledgments   87

I say that we are wound
With mercy round and round
As if with air
—GERARD MANLEY HOPKINS

|

THE ARTIST'S GARDEN AT GIVERNY

In my own small garden
magenta isn't a color
but a time of day

just before evening
when irises dab the air
bees gather

on the Russian sage
and the dark fruit
of the elderberry

fulfills its promise
at last / Years ago
I folded compost

into the soil
to build an opulent layer
over the dark

clay of the mountain
I terraced the earth
with stone

as I did in my father's garden
decades ago / Now
at the end of what I thought

I knew
white-tail graze the roses
Josie barks furiously at the window

and I rush into the garden
to chase deer away
like an old scarecrow

Monet painted the iris bed
only once
while devoting 30 paintings

to haystacks
250 to waterlilies
which his gardener cleaned

every morning
and 18 to the Japanese bridge
over the pond

He stationed easels around the shore
to work multiple
canvases

simultaneously
to catch the light
at different times of day

In his last years
as his vision failed
he was learning from theory

practice and memory
to see as I am learning
to see

magenta isn't a color
but a compromise
the eye makes between

red and green
so irises almost pink
almost blue

in dappled light
turn
green leaves red

while the artist's
house
glimpsed through the trees

burns
like a distant
fire

ZED

Somehow I came to believe if we live
faultless lives, kind and generous,
if we sit at the bedside of those who have
no one else, if we bend to rub the ears
of the dog hungry for small attentions,
rock the baby in our arms
so mom can sleep in the next room,
hours sliding by like gentle ghosts,
if we sit down with the small boy
and carve the alphabet to zed,
if we ask the name of the doll, held
so sweetly in the little girl's arms,
if we kindly lie, praising the bland dish
served with love as we visit the home
of an old friend, sit on the patio,
watch monarchs land on milkweed
halfway to the place ancient memory
calls home because we have no other life
than this one, if we remember the far boat
of long ago where a boy and an old man
cast their lines into the still water
of evening, if we are kind to ourselves
we can be kind to others, and then
we'll be protected. Our children will be safe.
We can leave this earth in peace.
Oh, my dear friend, I remember how you held
your baby in your arms as we sat in the grass
on a summer day, and we never imagined
we'd outlive our children

for N.S.

AGAINST PRAYER

Okay,
God of crib death
and dirty needles,
of heroin and fentanyl,
God of twisted steel
burning beside the road,
God of truncheon
and unholstered hatred,
God of the mob and the blood-
stained floor of the cell,
what do you want from me?

Forty years ago I fell
on my knees and asked you
to remove my craving.
Thief, drug dealer,
addict who'd steal
his mother's crutches
given the chance
I had no right to ask
yet the light grew
in the dark room,
a weight was lifted.
I walked into the bright
heat of a Dallas summer
and each face I passed
glowed with love.
       So I ask you now
if you can save
a thief and thug
like me why take these
sweet ones? Who
are you who gives
and withholds light?
What are we to you?

SCARECROW

When the scarecrow was new,
He wore an old shirt of my father's,
A pair of khakis from Goodwill,
A pair of shoes from Salvation
While his head full of rags
Was held by the strings
Of his neck. He didn't complain
When the tractor finished the rows
Of corn and he was left alone
To watch the green sprouts rise.
Growing taller by the day
They held up green hands
In supplication, whether to the sun
Or the stars we never knew

As necks grew long, flowers
Of tassels misted a powder
Blown by the wind and each one
Became pregnant with something
That looked to us like joy.
The scarecrow watched over
His congregation, even as wind
And storms tore at his clothes
And the crows grew to know
His indecisive guardianship,
Persisting on his cross of sticks
As lightning played in the air

IMPERFECT

My native tongue doesn't allow
the imperfect tense, so it's difficult
to say how something might used
to happen but no more. Elizabeth
used to walk among these trees.
She used to walk among these trees
but doesn't anymore. Elizabeth
is no more though she used to be.

My sister doesn't anymore but she used
to walk among these trees because
she used to be happy but only
for a short while before she descended
to despair. Elizabeth we could say
used to walk among these trees
because they made her happy.
Elizabeth used to be but no more

LEAVING WALDEN

Is it true the distance between atoms
is proportionate to the distance between stars
and the world we know is mostly empty space?

When electrons pass each other
do they entangle, keeping
a connection as they travel away,
a connection so close
they mirror each other's motion
even on opposite sides of the world?

If so, why did our mother leave us
and move to a city far away
where she said she was always cold?

*

I don't know my mother's last words
but my sister's were *I decide*

Henry David's last words were
Now comes good sailing
followed by two lone words *moose* and *Indian*
Henry David died at 44. My sister at 49.
Everyone dies soon enough.

Unlike Henry David, I often quarrel with God—
or at least the God I knew when I was young.
But this afternoon walking home
through a stand of sunlit mountain laurel
I pause to give thanks
for this one small life

ODYSSEUS IN HELL

My people call themselves *evangelical*
which means *good messenger*
the angel who arrives
with news of grace

The night my mother died
I couldn't sleep
I went downstairs
to make chamomile tea
and stare into darkness
When she came to me
I tried to embrace her

My people believe
you can be saved
if you ask
and what saved me years ago
from the hell of that house
was poetry / strange
angel that it was

Grace came
from the music of words
and God
if you want to call
a respite from torment
God was a character in a story
repeated so many times
it seemed true
like the story of gravity
or the face of the moon
looking down
with a love I wanted
to take for granted

My bookshelf was crowded
with poets who sang me
to sanity

Sitting in the dark hour
of my mother's death
I thought of Odysseus
descending into Hades
to speak to Tiresias
the blind seer

Wandering
through the underworld
our sly but unwise hero

stumbles across his mother
who asks why
he's come still alive to this place of shadow
He recounts his failure
to return home / Then he asks
how she died and she tells him
she died of grief
for him

My mother died of grief
as well / Oh Lord
my sister blew her brains out
in a bathroom in Llano, Texas
while her parents sat on the front porch
enjoying the morning light

And my mother carried that darkness,
trying to eat her way
back into the light
until her heart burst

My sister believed
no one loved her
while I believe
my mother loved me
and my father
despised me

I learned to live
with a half-filled hole
inside me / And then in the middle
of the middle of my life
I flew to Austin
and drove through the dry hills
to my mother's funeral

I thought of Odysseus
trying three times
to embrace his mother,
each time his arms
passing through her

I asked myself why
am I in this place of darkness
still alive and I answered
I'm lost and trying to return home
I've been lost a long time

though I was once saved
by poetry / You need
to understand
my people believe
you can be saved if you ask

My people believe
no matter what you've done
you can fall on your knees
and beg to be saved
but first you must believe

ω!

Outside our window, snow is falling
on the cliff, covering the roofs of houses,
church steeple, treetops, toys, bicycles,
ghosts of happier times.
On the radio, distant war.

I think of Bohr, Heisenberg, and Schrödinger
a century ago, watching their world crumble.
As if they'd stepped off the cliff and remained in the air
supported only by their faith
in mathematics, they were learning
to measure the immeasurable,
one proof leading to another,
the irrational leading to the transcendent.

Set theory led to the Absolute Infinite Ω,
a sequence larger than any conceivable
or inconceivable quantity, finite or transfinite—
more than all possibilities combined
and linked to the idea of God.

And Ω's little brother ω (or ω!)
uncountable, the primitive root of unity.
The first and smallest transfinite ordinal,
it describes an unseeable world
containing both real and imaginary numbers,
essential, impossible, proven.
The reality we know,
everything we touch and see,
is one of many.

The bright light of the blizzard in my window,
snow falling on my world,
this pen, this framed image in front of me

of a man in coat and tie at the bedside
of a drunk in a t-shirt
I keep to remind me of my recovery from despair,
of this home where we've raised our children,
cooked our meals, written our books, of these rooms
where I've sat beside a lamp ten thousand hours
reading great and not so great poets,
where I've slept ten thousand nights beside the woman I love—
the life I imagine I know.

USHANT (CONRAD AIKEN AT HIS DESK)

Imagine the boy hearing
gunshots and coming
downstairs to find his father
and mother dead—
and living
with this memory every quiet
moment, the left hand
of the past joining
the right hand of the present
in a single entity defined by
the joining of gunshots
in the mind of the man
now at his desk, the man always
returning to the image fixed
to the present with a half twist,
that two-dimensional
image sneaking into
the three-dimensional now
of Conrad, eldest son
of William and Anna
of Savannah, in a continuous
loop, a rhyme
repeating in his mind
like the single entity
of the marriage ending
with the doctor killing his wife,
killing himself, completing
the twisted Möbius path of his son
who remembers the sound
of two conjoined gunshots,
remembers then forgets
the unbearable terror of
seeing his parents lying
in blood on the floor
and the boy now a man
who stands over them,
always circling back

STRANGE MEADOWLARK

Although my father had perfect pitch
he said he hated music because when he was a boy
each time his mother emerged from the hospital
she'd sit and stare at the back garden,
then she'd slowly rise, go to the piano
and as her mania rose to a crescendo
she'd improvise long compositions
a neighbor once confused with Brahms.

Perhaps I can forgive my father for believing
children learn only through pain and humiliation.
Other than my grandmother's improvisations
no music was allowed in our home.

Only much later did I succumb to Flash
who used to noodle the piano at a bar in Iowa City
allowing me to improvise poems as he played.
One night we broke into the college auditorium
and I listened to his *Christmas Sonata* performed
on a baby grand in the dark where I felt invisible and free.

Flash showed me how Brubeck uses 9/8, 6/4, 5/4—
time signatures he learned from street musicians
performing folk songs in Istanbul. Eventually
Paul Desmond's *Take Five* in 5/4 became my anthem,
a beautiful ear worm I still hear whenever words fail me.

One evening I was listening
    to Brubeck's *Strange Meadowlark*
thinking how 1959 changed music forever
with *Time Out, Kind of Blue, Ah Um*
and *The Shape of Jazz to Come*
and how at the age of five I spoke my first words
but my tongue stuck to the top of my mouth
so every word sounded like *arrr, warrr, jarrrrr,*
and how years later jazz, a free communal experience
embodying love, saved me just as poetry saved me.

When my father called
without identifying himself
saying simply *I'm sorry*
I responded *Why? What have you done?*
Nothing nothing he said *I've done nothing*
I'm just calling to say I'm sorry for everything

I had to decide whether to say what I thought
of him, child abuser, chief tormenter
I'd spent my entire life trying to recover from,
or whether to forgive this dying man.

I took a deep breath and said *Listen*
when we were growing up we had food
on the table and a roof over our heads, you always
had a job, you didn't beat my mother, your kids
got as much education as they wanted. You did alright.
I know lots of fathers who didn't do as well.

When he went on to talk about a few of his abuses
against me, I minimized his crimes.
I was lying of course but we both knew he was dying
and I didn't want to send him off thinking I hated him
although I did and I found something surprisingly transcendent
about telling a difficult lie out of kindness. Which made me think

of Ornette Coleman playing a Grafton saxophone,
a cheap plastic instrument that flips
between dullness and harshness,
a novelty, a toy, not a serious instrument
but somehow Ornette makes the toy sing.
He creates harmony movement melody
free of any tonal center just as I had no center
for many years until I forgave my father
but then I began to miss my hatred of him,
that hole occupying the center of me for so long.

After my parents died the family gathered
beside the Llano River behind their house
where the current descends rapidly over the limestone shelf.
I held in my hand a few words of praise for my parents
but the words wouldn't form. My tongue
    stuck to the roof of my mouth.
I slurred a few words before nodding to my brother
who poured the ashes on the rapids as I heard
the soulful celebration of *Take Five* take to the air

A COWBOY IN THE CHAPEL OF BONES

Baby Head Cemetery, Llano, Texas

Where I come from
it's bad manners to speak of death
except in dead metaphors. *Kick the bucket. Bite the dust.*
Give up the ghost. Swan song—a pretty phrase, but bad ornithology.
I once heard a lady from London say *pop your clogs*
as if we throw off a pair of muddy shoes after a long walk in the rain—
not likely in the dusty streets of Llano, Texas,
where tooled boots Death might wear are the rage.

Cowboys are Calvinists.
We like the dead to stay dead,
ashes to ashes with no dust left over, no grave to visit.
Ancient cemeteries are just grazing land, undeveloped real estate
waiting its turn to be turned over to developers
of green and gold towers rising above the dry plains.
But our metaphors are a dead giveaway
that once we had more respect for the dead.
After all, a cliché is simply a beautiful phrase
we ride hot and put away wet until it weakens and dies.

*

On *Día de los Muertos*
my ex-in-laws visit the cemetery to party
with the dead, a celebration of mortality.
They laugh, eat, drink, wear tall masks of demons,
make gifts to the dead and the living alike,
skulls made of sugar and *pan de muerto* with frosting shaped like bones.

I love the *calaveras literarias*, irreverent epitaphs dedicated to the living.
Rudolfo, mourning his mother who stands alive in front of him, recites
Como extraño sus tamales, empanadas y atolito;
voy a tener que aprender a cocinar yo solito.
(He misses his mother because he hates his own cooking.)

To joke with death gives urgency to our lives.
When we remember what we'd rather forget
we see and speak more clearly.
Every day becomes an emergency, an emergence, *una aparición*
that forces us to become fierce about our faith,
to taste the chocolate before it melts,
to love the lover before love fades
and to honor the body with marigold before it rots.

*

Years ago in Portugal
I walked into the Chapel of Bones as if in a dream,
skulls, femurs, vertebrae cemented into walls,
three high windows casting a skeleton of light on the floor.
Our guide Virgilio told us the *Capela dos Ossos*
reminds us of the swift passage of life on earth.

No shit, I thought. *5,000 corpses*, he said,
peasants exhumed from Évora's medieval cemeteries,
bones arranged by the Franciscans in squares, spirals, pyramids,
a ceiling of white brick painted with black motifs.
Skulls scribbled with graffiti. Skeletons hanging from ropes.
Two desiccated corpses in glass cases, one a child.
Aonde vais, caminhante, acelerado?
Where are you going in such a hurry, traveler?

MOON PIE AND A FANTA

Time is no arrow but a pothole in the road
in front of the Valero Corner Stop in Llano, Texas
where I'm buying a Moon Pie and a Fanta
to feast the holy sacrament of high school
football in this town where a young woman
shot herself while her parents enjoyed
the spring morning and her husband fumed
over her saying goodbye, misunderstanding
her meaning

                where time keeps
circling back to *I should have been here*

where pink marble still flows
beside the river, boys still jump
off the dam, cars still cross the iron bridge
on their way to Cooper's BBQ and
anyone who'd remember her has died
or moved away like the days it takes
to drive anywhere I'd ever want to be

PRAYER TO ST. ANTHONY

Never mind the snows of yesteryear, Tony.
I want to know where my goddamned keys
walked off to this fine spring day
when pretty girls are sashaying past
the dragon cactus I planted next to
the driveway. I'm late for my appointment
to twist the vertebrae back to where they
used to be when the flowers of yesteryear
were still here begging to be smelled.
While you're at it, I'd like to have my hair
returned please, my short-term memory
shiny as a new nickel. Give me back
the thousands of stoned hours
watching stupid television
and the years spent on the patio behind
Milo Butterfinger's Saloon guzzling beer
beneath the palm trees of indolence.
I want to buy back the hours I was paid
mopping and painting the boiler room
floor of the Hilton on Mockingbird Lane.
I want my bowels pristine again,
my liver clean as a spring day
when cardinals sing and the traffic
in the sky is busy but moving along nicely.
I want to joke with my wild sister again,
hear her laugh, listen to my mother
speak of people she loved. I need
to warn the friends I lost to drugs
and jail. I need to stop hurting
for the people I've hurt, stop regretting
my regrets, the years gone like the money
I gambled in a crooked poker game
when I was fifteen. Tony, please return
the gifts I squandered. Let me revisit love,
the little flip my heart used to do when

Shawna Dietrich in chemistry class
smiled at me which come to think of it
wasn't often. Allow me to hitchhike
to Austin to hear Willie sing again.
Let me feel one more time the surefire rush
of catching a wave on a stolen surfboard
as Camille took the roof off
our house and carried it to sea
and I rode the long board to shore
a reckless nobody with nowhere to go

THINKING OF THE RAPTURE AT CASTRIOTA
METALS AND RECYCLING

I spent an hour
watching a crane
lower its giant arm
to a pile of scrap iron
lifting bundles
of wire mesh
shattered televisions
broken toaster ovens
spatulas scissors
frying pans fence posts
whole bags of rusty nails
even shoes hanging by
the metal aglets
at the tips of their laces

Leaving behind
the aluminum bones of lawn chairs
broken teeth of clay tiles
and a headless doll whose
one arm stretched toward me
as if I could save her

WHITE ROCK LAKE

On moonlit nights
my friends and I drove
the winding roads around

White Rock Lake
looking for the jilted girl
who drowned herself

and now walks the shore
in a sheer white dress
dripping wet,
asking strangers
for a ride

*

Only terrified Macbeth can see
the shade sitting in the king's place

at the head of the table,
the ghost who laughs
when Lady Macbeth
begs her husband to stop being

ridiculously dramatic:
Could they please just once
have a nice dinner

with friends? Welcome or not,
the dead intend to stay

*

Maria, 93, my wife's mother
sleeps with her sister Anneliese
long dead, so Maria

doesn't have to die alone.
What would you think if I said
a woman with blonde hair

and freckled face
you can't see
is sitting beside me now?

YOU VISIT MORE OFTEN NOW THAT
YOU'RE DEAD

For years I saw you only
every few years
though we spoke by phone
every few weeks
but now you come at night
when I wake from
long bike rides through
back roads of cane fields
in the bright sun
past the prison farm with
neat rows of vegetables
tended by men in
white suits / Innocent
you used to wave
not knowing they couldn't wave
back at you, the pretty blonde
gliding by smiling
in the beautiful days
before you were locked up
drug-crazed violent
ashamed of the videotapes
shown at the trial

You vowed so many times
to get clean / fly straight
find God / pretend to be happy
in a small Texas town
where you kept fireworks
hidden in the bathroom
next to the pistol / Now
you visit me / happy at last
or at least resigned to being
a trick of light free
of anger and confusion

You stand by the window
your face half in shadow
your tall thin athletic
body radiant / Death
becomes you
sister
as you knew it would

THE COLD

Everything dies, reborn
as something else
then dies again. Cicadas
sleep in their chambers
beneath the frozen grass.
Snow falls in the gutter.
The bees that crawled
over the purple sage
in summer now cluster
around their queen
to keep her warm.

I remember a boy
who couldn't speak
rocking in his chair
sucking his fingers
holding his bear
of no name, waiting
for his father to hit him
again. But inside
that dumbstruck child
it was summer
and he was singing like a bird

THE COVE

My grandfather used to take me
to a cove on a lake
in deep East Texas
where he taught me
to bait the hook with a worm
cast the line as far as I could
and wait in the shade
without casting
a shadow on the water

I did catch fish
usually small perch
we'd throw back.
My favorite part
was the quiet waiting
in birdsong
while small waves traced
the muddy shore.
A muskrat or moccasin
might swim by
barely noticing
our calm presence

I loved those mornings
of timeless simplicity.
I learned patience
is not something you work for
but something you wait for
deep below the surface
where the water weeds
move in slow darkness
and fish glide by
with a will of their own

WAVE

At sixteen I stole a surfboard
and drove to the shore
with my friends. In those days

we were young and stupid.
In those days we were sometimes happy.
Floating out

beyond the breakers
looking over our shoulders toward
the bright horizon, the ocean

rolling toward us
like the future, we were waiting
for the perfect wave

and when it came
I felt the great cylinder
of water lifting me

as the ocean rubbed against
the seafloor
breaking its forward motion

the wave curling into a tube
where we crouched, leaning
into our lives

as we rode to shore.
In the evening we built a fire
and girls in bikinis

sat with us
and someone with a guitar
teased a melody and someone

sang and I was vaguely
in love with everyone
and wanted nothing more

TRUST

When the treasurer of our group
got drunk and disappeared
we asked Jason to volunteer
for the job. Like a lot of the guys
Jason had done time, starting
as a juvie and continuing right up
to his release from Fayette
after eighteen months
for carrying a Ruger. Nobody
in the straight world
would trust Jason with their
money. Nobody. But we'd
seen Jason grow over
two years and he was
sponsoring other guys, mostly
ex-cons at Sunday
meetings, and often he shared a rage
and tenderness he said
he'd hadn't known
until his spiritual
awakening. *Bullshit*
Once a con always a con, right?
No. Sometimes a man changes,
not just stops lying
stealing hurting people
but his core changes and he
becomes somebody else.

And now my darling
I need you to know
when we first got married
35 years ago today
you trusted me with your money
and let me manage our finances
but you didn't know
I was a thief. I lifted

cigarettes and music tapes
from stores when I was a kid.
Once I boosted a surfboard
and I even stole my father's underwear
from his drawer when I was living
on the street and stopped by
for a shower and shave.
I lied so many times
I'd lost the truth and couldn't find
my ass with a map because I was high
every day. Then one day
in complete hopeless misery
I fell on my knees. I asked God
to relieve me of the bondage
of self. And He did. And for
the first time I knew who I was
and walked 20 blocks to a meeting
through the Dallas summer heat
and every face I saw appeared radiant
and I told everyone at the meeting
but no one seemed surprised.
As they recounted their own awakenings
each different than the other
I realized crawling out of a slippery hole
we've dug for ourselves happens all the time.
No need to keep lying, using and stealing.

And now my love after 35 years of
working and saving, look at us,
we're rich, that is,
we're comfortable and happy
in our love and now you say
you never regretted mingling
yours with mine. Thank you.

For Eva-Maria Simms on our 35th anniversary

BREATH

No one could enter the bathroom
where Elizabeth had shot herself, bits of bone
blood and brain everywhere.
We closed the door and tried not to think.

She felt unloved, but those of us who loved her
gathered at her house beside the Llano River
to mourn in our separate ways.
It was spring in the hill country
and bluebonnets covered the fields.

My sister's husband locked himself in his room for days
kept alive by my mother handing glasses of water
through a cracked door.
My sister's sons sat around a fire pit
with their friends, dazed teenage boys
crouching by the embers, refusing tears.

We brothers stunned and helpless, trying to be helpful
around the house, kept breaking things
cursing and crying. After an unbearable silence
Bob said *it's a hell of a thing, isn't it?*
A hell of a thing.

I remember walking into the Baptist church
standing at the back of the sanctuary
seeing a hundred people,
wondering who they all were,
so many Latinos with their children,
strangers at my sister's funeral.
Then I remembered my brothers had married
Latinas, generous people,
family I didn't know,
who surely loved my sister.

As children we were taught to hate Mexicans
and now we were Mexicans.
I started laughing, then wheezing uncontrollably,
panic rushing though me in waves.
Faces I didn't know turned to look at me
not unkindly, but with concern
and my nephew Andrew Narvaez,
a sweet kid I liked, took me gently by the arm
through the red doors of the sanctuary
to stand in the shade at the edge of the parking lot
beneath the wide arms of a live oak tree.

He stood silently beside me
until I could weep.
We waited for the others—
my brothers, my parents,
our large Mexican family
merging quietly and driving off
into the soft blue hills.

When we pulled into the driveway,
a woman was putting a mop and bucket
in the trunk of her car. She came to us,
hugged my mother and said quietly.
I'm so sorry, Janie Lu. We all loved her.

In the house, the bathroom door was open,
the light on, the surfaces immaculately scrubbed.
The neighbor whose name I didn't know
had come to the house unbidden
to scour tile and porcelain, to pick
bits of bone from the floor,
to wipe up smears of brain,
to clean blood-spray from the ceiling,
to wash every sign of self-murder away.

People say the world is an ugly place and maybe it is
but sometimes people are so damned kind
I can barely breathe.

AMERICA

Beside the highway outside McKeesport, PA,
a state trooper has pulled over a Black man
who leans against his rusty Ford
palms flat, feet apart
assuming the position
as we say in America

The smokey wears his broad-brimmed hat low
with its menacing chin strap
which is leather, like the leather of his boots
and belt and holster,
his face in shadow

Beside us, the Monongahela River
quickens, making its way
through abandoned pastures
and ruined river towns
on its way to the Ohio

As the smokey rummages through
the car, the man shrinks in his clothes,
catches my eye, then looks down
ashamed. *"What's he done?"* I wonder
"What's the trooper done?"

What have I done,
what have I ever done,
but look away / up the road
toward the beautiful Laurel Highlands
hidden in the white mist of America?

NIGHT SCHOOL

I used to teach policemen
at the community college—diligent, respectful, curious,
the only students who craved grammar lessons
because they knew their dialect marked them
as *Yinzers* from the Mon Valley.

One evening I showed up early.
Three students sporting chinos and cologne,
smelling for all the world like stockbrokers
on their day off, didn't notice me.

They were laughing
about an *ass whoopin* they'd delivered
to a Black kid the night before.

As the cops took turns beating him,
the *boot*, as they called the rookie,
broke a bone in his hand.

Bill, the gray one they called *Sarge*, said
Son, never hit a guy with your fist.
Carry a sap. Use the tools of the trade.

Most cops like truncheons
for the intimidation factor Sarge said
But I like a tool I can carry in my pocket

He pulled out
a leather sack of lead pellets
and slapped it on his palm.

Hitting the skull, spine, groin or sternum
is considered deadly force—illegal
Sarge warned
but we do it all the time

*

I remember walking home at 2 a.m. from a bar
in Iowa City, joining an angry crowd surrounding
a policeman beating a man crouched in the street
begging for mercy, hands protecting his face.

The cop, intent on his work,
hadn't noticed the crowd until he looked up startled
put his hand on his holster and ordered us to disperse.
Then he bundled the man into the squad car and drove off.

The next day at the police station
a captain politely nodded, took a few notes,
thanked me for my citizen's report,
then shook my hand and assured me
he *would* investigate and be in touch.

I believed him. I was very young.

Since then, I've often wondered
how it feels to think of oneself
as the hammer of justice.
How does it feel to inflict pain
as a joyful act
of public service, an obligation,
a jubilation, almost
a prayer?

*

Last week I ran into Sarge on a street corner.
He'd retired from the force, lost weight
and stopped drinking. He said he was happy
teaching his grandkids how to fish.

I still didn't want to like him
but I did. We were just

two old white guys standing on the sidewalk
talking about stuff.

Later I thought about Sarge
all those years ago in my classroom
explaining how to beat a suspect in handcuffs.

When I remembered the ecstasy
on his ruddy face
I hated him all over again.

HOW MY BROTHER TRIED TO SAVE US

Forty-four years ago, when my brother Ken confronted
our sister's boyfriend Gary, and the lowlife
took a wild swing at him, Ken ducked.

The blow hit him on the forehead
knocking him down and breaking Gary's hand.
The pimp, who'd been selling our sister
to his friends, ran away crying.

My father joked
when I told you to use your head, Ken,
I didn't mean like that.
My brother said, *Well I didn't lose the fight.*

But he did lose. We all lost.

As revenge for betraying him
Gary kidnapped Elizabeth
and kept her in a cage for weeks,
farming her out until he broke her

*

Reader, this is not a metaphor.
This is the world I come from.
My sister was literally kept in a cage
and raped repeatedly.

Elizabeth didn't tell us for twenty-five years.
By then, she was ready to die.

*

Elizabeth's suicide broke my mother,
and it nearly broke me
but my father never spoke of it.
Nor did Ken.

The two men seemed unsurprised
as if they were so beaten down
there was nothing more life could do to them.

I'm not sure what broke my father.
A crazy mother maybe.
Or maybe just being an average American guy
overworked and frightened.

As for Ken, he hasn't spoken to me
since his last suicide attempt
six years ago

*

As we sat in the visitor's room
of the psych hospital
Ken, his wrists bandaged, told me
a few months before Dad died
Ken had confronted the old man
about the way he treated me
when I was small

He said Dad had chuckled
Well maybe at times I went a little too far

My brother responded *you didn't go a little too far
You abused him because you enjoyed it
and you knew you could get away with it
because he couldn't speak*

A few days later, Dad called me to apologize.
Sobbing, he tried to explain his life to me
but there's no explaining what's in a man's heart
when he hurts someone just because he can

NO

To Vladimir Putin

No is the place we go when yes has been all used up.

No is waking from darkness, returning to a blessed country from a bad dream.

No is the rhythm of assertion, the hammer of refusal, the long pause before acceptance of the coming battle.

No is the full stop, coming to sense after a foolish year.

No is the extinguished fire, the frame around the picture, the inviolable border.

It is the slapped hand, the hard stare, the nostrils flared.

No is the single syllable growing to a roar, stomping the ridiculous, the insulting, the oppression of the bully and the evil of the rapist.

No is not nothing. When everything has been taken from you, no is all you have left.

No is an affirmation of the right to hold out, the refusal to let go.

No is the pile of dust swept out, floors scrubbed raw, skin blistering with the sun of *yes-boss* said too long.

It is shade on a summer's day, the respite of the tired hero.

No is a pause, a re-set, a do-over, a redoubt, a change of direction that is not your yes on your terms.

No is not maybe. No means not ever, no way, not this way, no sirree bub, hit the road Vlad, shut your pie-hole, Donny.

HALL OF BLOOD

After the men had removed to the field
the bodies of the suitors
dismembered them
and fed them to the pigs

the twelve servant girls
the murdered men had raped
were called
to the hall still slick with blood

to scrub the marble floors
pick bits of brain from the walls
throw ropes of intestine
in slop buckets to be taken to the barn

And even
on this first morning
laughter again visited
the kitchen / Dogs wandered
through rooms without fear
of being kicked

The servant girls trusted
they'd been forgiven / hoped
their children's children
would ask to hear songs
of their ancestral king
Odysseus Killer of Men

but that day
as the girls worked
to make order again
to mop away signs
of slaughter / no one spoke
except in whispers
not to invite return
of unwelcome shades

THE MACHINERY

Steers smell blood in the slaughterhouse and panic
while we calmly stroll the aisles of the supermarket
gently placing plastic-wrapped flesh in our baskets

While we sleep, a tugboat tows our garbage scow
of bones and plastic out to sea

THE SENTENCE

After sentencing four young women
for placing water jugs in the desert,
the judge returns to his chambers,
removes his black robes
and puts his face in his hands.
Behind him, law books stare down—
sentries on the walls of a crumbling city.

BROTHERLY LOVE

AWP conference, Philadelphia, March 2022

I broke from the colloquy of ten thousand poets,
walked down Arch Street with the March wind
in my face and a few flakes falling. I was headed

for dinner but, as things turned out, I became a witness
to love. Evening filled the air with light and shadow.
Two young men walked toward me holding hands—

the air was cold but the men were warmed by laughter.
A stylish older couple passed by arm in arm,
their faces pink and happy in their woolen scarves.

I walked past the Kabuki Sushi and the TexMex Grill,
past the elegant Notary Hotel with its marble floors
and mirrored halls where we'd discussed Dickinson,

past the magnificent City Hall in the Second Empire style
of 88 million red bricks and thousands of tons of white marble,
over 700 rooms and 250 sculptures, capturing artists,

educators, and engineers who embodied American ideals
and contributed to this country's genius as the bronze says
and the tall clock tower, witness to the slow decay

of this glorious city of brotherly love and anguish.
I came to the *Fogo de Chão* Brazilian Steakhouse
on Chestnut Street where a great haunch of roasted calf

is carved beside each table and I tried not to think
of the terrified yearling who'd given his life for this spectacle
of consumption. Not having tasted flesh for 15 years,

I filled up on fresh greens, beans, fruit and light fluffy
pão de queijo at the lavish salad bar
and my young friends and I laughed and gossiped

and ranted about the current war and the past president
and who'd won the big-ass poetry prize
and whether someone else, meaning one of us,

should've. Next, the U-Bahn with live loud music
by SlamJam but I couldn't hear anyone talking,
hadn't had a drink in 37 years, too old for sloppy,

and my friends were heading to the Good Dog Bar
The Black Sheep Pub or the Harp and Crown—
they couldn't decide—so I said goodbye and walked away,

calling it a night after 68 years of mostly good luck
and walked up Filbert toward 13th where it passes
beneath the Convention Center, the wind becoming fiercer

and the snow faster and harder, white in the darkness.
People hunched over as they walked,
holding their collars close around their throats

and I remembered going to the Flower Show
at the Convention Center the day before
where the air was heavy with jasmine and gardenia

and I thought heaven if it's anything at all
must surely and entirely be warmth, scent and color.
I turned onto 13th Street, a block-long tunnel

where people sleep on the sidewalk huddled in blankets
and plastic sheets, hoodies hiding their faces,
their hands neither black nor white but gray

with the dust of the city, a few zombie drug addicts
but mostly just people with nowhere to sleep
except this dark cold cave their lives had become.

A man with a puppy snuggling inside his coat
glanced up, puzzled. People like me usually walk
the long way around to avoid people like him

because we're afraid to look deprivation
in the eye, resent admitting our own dumb luck,
but in my superior compassion, my arrogant morality

I decided to risk walking among the indigent
as if I were Mother Teresa and not just a tourist
of misfortune. A car stopped. A white woman

in jeans handed a Styrofoam box
to a man hunkered and trembling on the sidewalk.
He nodded thanks and the car moved to the next man

and the next, each one receiving supper,
perhaps a Last Supper I thought wryly, immediately
ashamed of finding irony in compassion.

The car came to a woman with two small girls,
the mother dressed in rags but her children in pink parkas,
the woman giving everything to her children,

keeping nothing for herself, and the small family
received the dole of fried chicken, mashed potatoes,
brown gravy, a dinner roll, a small heap of chopped greens

and a delicate plastic fork, tines breaking off
in their food. The car pulled up
to the last man standing on the sidewalk,

gray hoodie pulled back revealing a scarred face,
dreadlocks like a black halo.
The social worker handed him his dinner

and the man leaned over to kiss her cheek,
a chaste thank you, an affectionate reward
for her kindness, but the woman yanked

her head back, avoiding his kiss
and the two stood surprised,
their faces a hand's breadth apart,

two travelers caught in a web, uncertain
how to break loose from the other's gaze.

IV

FAYE DONNELLY EXPLAINS WHY THE DEAD
ARE IN OUR LIVES

Faye seems happy with her room
in the nursing home *Good light*
she says wheeling toward the window
smiling at the sky *Here's*
my new painting called *Sentience*
gesturing at a canvas on a tripod
Do you see it?

As I'm looking at the painting
it changes / An incoherent mass
of color arranges itself around
my seeing / Flowers emerge
Beasts of all kinds / Clouds
and distances and surprises
and impertinence and the sense
something large is being unsaid
the way babble emerges
from raw sound
to become a child's
kernel of the world

Wow is all I can say / Faye smiles
reaffirming her intuition that
something that's there / is

*

I was so sorry to hear about
your sister Faye says
It must be painful
for you to remember
Yes I say *it's an open wound*
I carry with me
I think of her every day
how she laughed
how we joked

she always claimed
I was the only one who could
make her laugh

That's a big responsibility
Faye says *To carry
someone's joy
Grief is heavy and easy
to hold onto
but joy escapes us*

Yes I say *Grief
is heavy and joy escapes me*
and I sit down next to Faye
Is it difficult for you I ask
*being in a wheelchair
living in this one room?
You used to travel and you
loved your job at the library
Do you feel confined?*
Oh no Faye says *I'm happy here
I'm grateful for my wheelchair
Imagine how many
people had to work together
with their hands and minds
and spirits to bring this
machine to me! And
my window brings me
the serene morning
All day pigeons and sparrows
rest on the sill / How strange
they cannot see me
just a few feet away
little souls
who'll carry me away
soon* Faye looks at me
*I'm quite happy Michael
but you are not*

No I am not I say
Your grief is a burden
you've carried a long time
Faye says *How long has it been since*
Elizabeth died? Thirteen years
I answer *She committed suicide*
thirteen years ago in April
She died in the spring?
How wonderful to die
when life is coming back
Faye says. She sees my flash of anger
You must let go of her
you know / I know
I say. *She wouldn't want*
you to suffer you know
Faye says / *Yes I know*
I say *but how do I let go of my grief?*
First Faye says *you must recognize*
she's still with you
She's beside you now
You can see her? I ask
I can see the darkness you carry
Faye says *You hold onto it*
because you miss her
and because you feel guilt
for her death.
Yes I say *she called me*
a few weeks before she killed herself
We hadn't talked in a year
after a falling out and finally
she called and we joked
and laughed like we used to
The last thing we each said
was I love you / She did love you
Faye says *She was giving you*
a gift forgiving you /
I abandoned her when she
needed me I say

Is that true Faye asks
or did you abandon each other?
We abandoned
each other but I should have—
What? Faye asks *what*
could you have done?
She was choosing to die
That was her right
No one has the right
to take a life not even her own
I say. I am weeping.
Can you see her? I ask again
No Faye says *I cannot see her*
any more than I can see
the wind but I can see
the presence of the wind
in the trees the way
it carries leaves down
the street below my window
When the nurse
rolls me into the garden
I can feel the breeze
on my cheek
I can feel the air
as I breathe and the strength
it gives me so no
I cannot see the immanence
of your sister but
you can feel her with you
and now it is time
to let her leave and soon
it will be time to let me leave as well

*

When my sister first came back
she was nothing more
than a whisper like a breeze

in the leaves but later her voice
grew stronger and I heard
her laughing gently when I
was angry and she put her
hand on my arm to reassure
and I wasn't frightened
by her presence but worried
for my sanity which had never
been shall we say robust
so I ask Faye what she
thinks about ghosts and
she says they're real because
we make them then doubt
them / *So my sister is real*
because I want her
beside me? I ask and Faye
says *Yes we bring back people*
we love when we need them
the way we see what we want
to see in the mirror sometimes and
tell ourselves what is barely
true and leave out a lot
And I say *but leaving out the fact*
that someone is dead
is over the top don't you think?
And Faye thinks
for a moment and says
Not necessarily
it depends on whether
you think death is a permanent
unchangeable fact or
simply a transitory state
like water
evaporating from a lake
later becoming rain and Faye
points at a husk
of a locust on the path
where I'm pushing

her chair beneath the summer
maples / *Is it dead or alive* she asks
It's dead I answer *but it once*
was part of a living thing
Yes Faye says *it's still part*
of a living thing everything
is alive the stone the dirt
the air the water and especially
the breath your breath is alive
it is spirit it is life it is the raw
stuff of our godlike being and
your sister is still with you
in your mind your body your
experience everywhere you
go she is with you and sometimes
you know it and feel it and sometimes
not but stop here on this path
Take my hand close your eyes
and let's just breathe together
and listen to all the living
breath of the world and yes
the tree is alive and
the stone and the wind
deep inside the stone
is the mind
of the stone and deep
inside the wind is the mind
and deep inside you
is the mind inside your mind
and there your sister is
with you so breathe with her
and let her speak

*

After Faye died
Eva the true gardener and I
followed the flat stones

of the path through
the azaleas
roses zinnia sage
past the spice garden
the spiral of lettuces
and the compost bin
with its dark
promise (whether my Crohn's
has finally turned cancerous
is knowledge waiting
its time)

Faye painted pink magnolia
fuchsia on twisting branches
chickadees perching
fireflies circling
in their own light
These paintings like Faye herself
spill over boundaries
Upstairs in Eva's study
we hang another painting
not a celebration
but a mystery
a large portrait entirely
in red and black
a man's face wreathed
in oak leaves / his black beard knotted
with ribbons / his eyes fierce
an earth spirit
all muscles and exuberance

WATERFALL

In Chatham Woods near our house
a spring bursts
from a hillside and falls
into a rocky pool
beside a small wooden bridge
where I like to stand
to watch the water
spill down the hillside
drowning
the zigzag path
to the open cave
of the storm sewer beside
the highway and from there
no doubt it flows to Sawmill Run
curving down the southern hills
to merge with the Monongahela
and Ohio
and Mississippi and from there
the sea / Yes
I can travel beyond
my body but
why not stay here
with choke cherry and service berry
native to these hills
with sumac and silver birch
from God knows how far away
I've grown roots
in the soil of this mountain but I know
I am invasive.
I take more than I need.
I burn my way
through a place I barely belong
as I barely belong in this poem
if that's what you want
to call this

tumbling down
the stairs this dancing
of an old man in the evening
of his life

UNIVERSAL BEAUTY

Clicking on a Beard Butter ad
I'm directed to Universal Beauty
where a stunning woman with red lips
and bare shoulders says
Spike it. Scrunch it. Sleek it.
She looks past me to the young me
when I grew my first mustache
and a friend's wife said I was now
less beautiful and more delectable

I study the Moroccan Argan oil
which promises to *boss up your beard*
the Black Castor Oil
applied hot to soften the skin
and the Jamaican Mango Lime gel
to *give in to your whim*

My whim, young beauty, is to fly
to Antigua, the island of my youth,
to sit in the shade of a palm while steel-drum music
drifts in the breeze

                    but youth has long flown away.
My beard is gray, my hair sparse and universal beauty rests
neither in the mirror, nor the past, but only
in the elegant symmetry of waves
that lap eternity's shores

SIDEWALK DRAIN WITH MOSS AND STRING

If it's human
to put things in a category
like putting them in a bag

a few pebbles collected in the alley
for their odd striations of color
you imagine forged in a volcano
when molten mass was a thing around here

a tattered notebook with a few scribbles
you wrote after your mother died

a hatband, a rubber band, a hairclip
dropped by a girl you were afraid to speak to

and out of the whole deck you saved only
the Jack of Spades winking at you knowing
something about you keeps changing

if this hoarding of memories
is what makes you human then
are crows our cousins

carrying bits of yarn and bottle caps
to their nests weaving shiny things
into their homes the way
you brought home a photo

of a sidewalk drain full of green moss
two pink roots curving onto the aggregate
on one of the roots a piece of string
because happiness clings to small things?

THE SIMPLE HEART

I prefer the simple heart with its
Clear glass bells and violets spilling
From the clouds but what I get is
This mud-caked boot disguised as
A flowerpot and this abominable
Meal of tse-tse and by-byes as
If I were wanting wanting wanting
So bad anything would do but it
Won't damnit I need you beside me
As firmly as the bad luck I've carried
Because you my dear are your own
Prepossessing self, not mine

JOY

Joy is a foreign language to me.
The way it trips into the room *with* a care in the world,
Letting the dog drool, the baby sleep, the woman weep
As she remembers the kindness of her father.

Joy is a stranger who comes to the door
With small gifts and a big soul.

My friend Valerie fills the room with laughter,
Leaving no one out, no one at a loss.
Everyone is praised for their imperfections.

Joy is a language she speaks with ease
And teaches me to speak from deep in my chest,
The guttural rumblings of knowing
How things have gone wrong for the best

JUBILATE

Now I shall praise our dog Josie
the bodhisattva of our household

the perfect embodiment
of devotion, always present
in spontaneous awe

quietly happy with her bowl and leash
the warm circle of her bed of contentment

fierce to defend her family
accepting of guests, at peace
with knowing herself, rejoicing in the good

gnawing on the bone of persistence
rejoicing in the belly-rub of pleasure
forgiving insults, abandoning resentments

never withholding love
incapable of lying
licking the face of puppy and master alike

With her, we devote ourselves
to the religion of kindness
tendering attention on each moment

Aspiring to bliss, we awaken to the real
We relish our dinner. We accept the lead

We delight in the squeaky toy
of the tv remote, the rawhide chew of politics
the tussle and chase of debate

After a day of work and play
I lay my head on your lap
beside the open window of our home

where the elderberry brings the cardinal
and the butterfly bush invites the monarch
and I rest in the wisdom of Dog

PUPA (a meditation on becoming)

We think of metamorphoses
as glorious and beautiful,
quiescent

chrysalis emerging
as a yellow butterfly
that slowly unfolds her

translucent wings
to let them dry
in the open air

then flying off
in a flittering arc
reminding us

of our emergence from
the chrysalis of self-conscious
adolescence

into the less tumultuous
uncertainties
of adulthood and of

the final transformation
we yearn for, the moldering body
releasing the immortal spirit, but imagine

how the wormlike
caterpillar feels after a life
of happily munching leaves

to curl herself
on the underside of a chosen leaf
to secrete a fiber

spin a cocoon, incorporating
twigs, urticating hairs,
fecal pellets, bits of leaf and bark

to disguise herself from
predatory bats and nightjars
while the arrival works its magic.

But if she's aware
as all things are aware—
rock, tree, wind—

she must feel
her skin stretching, covering
her body now

a thing with wings
that doesn't resemble
hope so much

as grace, the undeserved love
that comes into our lives
as a gift. And I

as always thinking only
of myself
project onto this insect

my puerile
theology of desire
as she changes from an ugly

esurient creature
pain coursing like green blood
through every cell

a foreign essence assuming
her body while I want to
welcome a spirit

untamed, unguarded
unprotected, unrestrained
as she sprouts furled wings

and the sharp-edged leafcutter
mouth elongates to a spiral tongue
for sucking nectar.

Surely she is oblivious
to the accidental perfection
of her beauty, a lesson and a gift

for me, for all of us. Aristotle
named the butterfly
Psyche to evoke

the ravishing princess who aroused
Cupid's passion
and Aphrodite's jealousy

the mother commanding
her son to inspire in Psyche
desire

for the most despicable
of men, that on a bad day
would be me of course

so I'm grateful to the soul of love
the father of science
projected onto this caterpillar

which the Greeks named
chrysalis meaning
gold

for the way light
catches
the dew-covered casing and

Linnaeus the father of taxonomy
called this post-larval stage,
the adolescence of the insect

if you will, *pupa*, Latin
girl, doll, puppet
related to *pupil, puberty, pubescence*

reminding me
of my daughter years ago
tearing free

from her adolescent shell
and flying away
full of grace

leaving behind *Felicity*
her favorite doll
and *Sebastian*

the puppet
her mother made, lifted into life
with no voice of his own

his body
controlled by wires
from above, his ineffectual

wooden hands, his painted eyes
rolling in hollow sockets
witness to my daily

decay, my flesh
absorbing and releasing
my bones dissolving

my entire skin replaced
every few weeks,
my breath

spiritus
in constant emergence
because I'm not a solid body

but a location
and my spirit if it exists
as more than metaphor

invented by my hubris
and fear of dying
wants to know

does it return to the source?
Is there a wave
I'm riding to shore

a breath of wind
carrying me in erratic flight
above the field of flowers?

CODA: THE CROWS

We barely recognized ourselves
But the crows knew
Who we were and where we'd been
Why we returned
Without meaning to
Perhaps they recognized our regret
As theirs, or perhaps it was just
We had changed everything
But our faces
Which we held in place
With effort, not wanting
To admit how wrong we'd been
How far away

Notes

The Artist's Garden at Giverny: In 1890–91, Claude Monet painted haystacks thirty times to capture the quality of light in different seasons. Later, he bought a nearby meadow, dredged it to plant waterlilies, built a Japanese bridge and painted it eighteen times before painting one view of the iris garden in 1900, *The Artist's Garden at Giverny.* The same year he embarked on two major projects—a series of the River Thames in London and another series of his waterlilies which he painted two hundred and fifty times, a project that occupied the next twenty years. I am fascinated by his painting of the iris garden not only because the painting is beautiful but also because it stands as a singularity, a small lyric among his epic sequences.

Imperfect: My autism sometimes causes me to get stuck on a sentence I'll repeat again and again with minor variations. I was writing an elegy about the trees near my sister's house, but I couldn't capture the feeling-memory. Then, I realized what I needed was the past imperfect tense—a past action performed repeatedly—but English doesn't have the imperfect tense. Later, I saw that my failed attempts to find the right phrase were themselves a small ode to imperfection.

Odysseus in Hell: The Odyssey, Book 11.

ω!: Omega (upper case Ω, lower case ω), the last letter of the Greek alphabet, has various meanings in different disciplines. In set theory, ω (or ω!), pronounced oh (or oh!) is the first infinite ordinal number after the natural numbers (1, 2, 3, 4, 5...) and it includes all numbers that come before it. The ordinal numbers are counted as $\omega + 1$, $\omega + 2$, $\omega + 3$.... Ω denotes the set of all countable ordinals, in other words, all the numbers that come after the natural numbers. These concepts are useful to theoretical physicists in imagining the infinity of space/time. The concept of ordinal numbers was first put forward by the German mathematician Georg Cantor, the creator of set theory, in 1883 to accommodate infinite sequences.

Ushant (Conrad Aiken at His Desk): The title of Conrad Aiken's autobiographical novel *Ushant* refers to the rocky island in the British Channel which is a traditional starting point for navigations around the globe, as well as a metaphor for the memory of a tragedy that happened in Aiken's childhood. On February 27, 1901, Aiken's father, a respected eye surgeon in Savannah, Georgia, shot his wife Anna and then killed himself in the family home. Their oldest child Conrad, 11 years old, was in his bedroom and hearing the shots came downstairs and discovered the bodies of his parents.

Prayer to St. Anthony: St. Anthony of Padua (1195–1231), the most celebrated of St. Francis of Assisi's followers, had the reputation of a miracle worker and is often invoked as the patron saint of lost things. However, many suggest he is more importantly the patron of lost souls.

No: Written a few days after the invasion of Ukraine by Russia in February 2022.

Hall of Blood: The Odyssey, Book 19. After the slaughter of the suitors, Odysseus observes that he has only a few household chores left to tend to. He asks Eurycleia to identify the maidservants who were disloyal. A dozen are called in to clean the gore from the great hall—after which they are taken to the courtyard and hanged. The maidservants "kicked up heels for a little—not for long."

The Sentence: In January 2019, a federal judge found four women guilty of trespassing in a national wildlife refuge as they sought to place food and water in the Arizona desert for migrants. The four were volunteers for No More Deaths, which said in a statement the group had been providing life-saving aid to migrants. The volunteers who were convicted were Natalie Hoffman, Oona Holcomb, Madeline Huse and Zaachila Orozco-McCormick.

America, Night School, How My Brother Tried to Save Us, The Sentence, and *Brotherly Love* were originally published as a long poem *Original Sin* as part of *In Sheep's Clothing: The Idolatry of White Christian Nationalism,* edited by George Yancy and Bill Bywater (Springer, 2023) with this abstract:

> In the five cantos of *Original Sin*, I describe incidents of police brutality, child abuse, rape, slavery, forced prostitution, denial of refugee status, and criminalization of acts of conscience, as well as my own blithe assumption of privilege, which are presented as examples of the Original Sin of dehumanization out of which all other sins arise. The argument of the poem is that racism, sexism, and classism—and the resultant poverty, humiliation and violence—arise from rejection of one's *Inner Light* in the Quaker sense and *suffering resulting from separation* in the Buddhist sense, also known as *dehumanization of the other* in contemporary social theory. (See, for example,

the work of Nour Kteily, a psychologist at Northwestern University whose research is about dehumanization, our acquired ability to see fellow men and women as species inferior to ourselves.) I might add that everyone in Western society has developed this ability to objectify others. Even the good-hearted social worker in *Brotherly Love,* the last canto, is disgusted by a homeless man trying to give her a chaste thank-you kiss, rejecting the intimacy of his gesture because it would break down the caste-wall between them.

Universal Beauty: Nobel laureate Frank Wilczek's groundbreaking work in quantum physics was inspired by his intuition to look for a deeper aesthetic in the universe. He argues that this quest for the principles of Universal Beauty has guided the work of all great thinkers in the Western world, from Sappho to Einstein, and shows us how our ideas about perception, beauty and art are deeply entwined with our scientific understanding of the cosmos. *Universal Beauty* is also the name of a company that markets skin care products for men.

Acknowledgments

Thank you to the following publications and editors:

The Asheville Poetry Review (Keith Flynn): 'Strange Meadowlark'

The Banyan Review (Tayve Neese): 'Leaving Walden' as 'Steps,' 'Odysseus in Hell'

Invasion of Ukraine 2022, anthology (Richard Levine and Michael T. Young): 'No'

Live Encounters (Mark Ulyseas & David Rigsbee): 'The Cove,' 'Waterfall,' 'Wave,' 'You Visit More Often Now That You're Dead,' 'Thinking of the Rapture at Castriota Metals and Recycling,' 'Breath'

The Nonconformist (F.R. Foksal): 'No,' published in Poland and the United States

ONE ART: a journal of poetry (Mark Danowsky): 'A Cowboy in the Chapel of Bones,' 'America,' 'Sidewalk Drain with Moss and String'

Poem-a-Day, Academy of American Poets (Naomi Shihab Nye): 'Imperfect'

Rune (John Lawson): 'Coda: The Crows'

The Prism (Djelloul Marbrook, Kevin Swanwick): 'Imperfect' republished from Poem-a-Day; discussion of poem included

Scientific American (Dava Sobel): 'Pupa (a meditation on becoming)'

—

'America,' 'Night School,' 'How My Brother Tried to Save Us,' 'The Sentence,' and 'Brotherly Love' were originally published as a long poem 'Original Sin' in *White Christian Nationalism: An Inquiry,* edited by George Yancy and Bill Bywater (Springer, 2023).

Four lines from 'No' were displayed as part of the exhibit *Dear Ukraine* curated by David Hassler at the Center for Prayer and Pilgrimage at the National Cathedral in Washington, DC.

Some of the poems in this collection have been included in my blog 'Note from the Editor' published by *Vox Populi*.

Some of these poems have been translated into Arabic by Saleh Razzouk and published in the following magazines:

Al Quds Al Arabi, Arabic Jerusalem (daily, London),
Al Aalam, The World (daily, Baghdad),
Al Mothaqaf, The Intellect (e-zine, Australia)
Al Nakded Al Iraqi (e-zine, Istanbul).
PoetsPub (e-zine, Kuwait)

—

I am grateful to Ellen Foos, Arlene Weiner and Sandy Solomon for their close and patient editing of these poems, to Pamela L. Schnitter for designing this book, and to Naomi Shihab Nye, James Crews and Danusha Laméris for their ongoing inspiration.

Eva-Maria Simms listened to each of these poems, sometimes in multiple drafts, and offered suggestions and encouragement that made this collection possible. Thank you, my love.

MICHAEL SIMMS, who identifies as a person with autism, is the founder of *Vox Populi*, an online forum for poetry, politics and nature, as well as Autumn House Press, a publisher of books. He's the author of four full-length collections of poetry including *American Ash* and *Nightjar* (Ragged Sky, 2020, 2021), two novels including *Bicycles of the Gods: A Divine Comedy*, the co-author of a college textbook about poetry—and the lead editor of over 100 published books, including the best-selling *Autumn House Anthology of Contemporary Poetry*, now in its third edition. In 2011, the Pennsylvania Legislature awarded Simms a Certificate of Recognition for his contribution to the arts. Born and raised in Texas, Simms lives in the historic Pittsburgh neighborhood of Mount Washington with his wife Eva and their kelpie Josie.